Lo, the turquoise horse of Johano-Ai,
How joyous his neigh.
There on precious hides outspread standeth he,
There on tips of fair fresh flowers feedeth he,
There he spurneth dust of glittering grains,
How joyous his neigh.

The Turquoise Horse

Prose
&
Poetry
of the
American Indian

Selected by
Flora Hood

Pictures by
Marylou Reifsnyder

G. P. PUTNAM'S SONS • NEW YORK

My thanks go to—
Barbara Lucas, my editor at G. P. Putnam's Sons, and Faye Cantrell, my accurate, patient and enthusiastic typist, and her young son, Jeffrey

Text copyright ©1972 by Flora Hood
Illustrations copyright ©1972 by Marylou Reifsnyder
All rights reserved. Published simultaneously
in Canada by Longmans Canada Limited, Toronto.
Library of Congress Catalog Card Number: 72-81586
SBN: GB-399-60744-7
SBN: TR-399-20292-7
PRINTED IN THE UNITED STATES OF AMERICA
All Ages

In memory of my brother, Carl,
his adopted son, Earl,
and his wife's Blackfoot mother of Canada
&
To my friends:
Dr. J. B. Wilbanks and Aline Lankford of Georgia,
Elizabeth Turpen of Albuquerque and Mary Lathrop of San Francisco

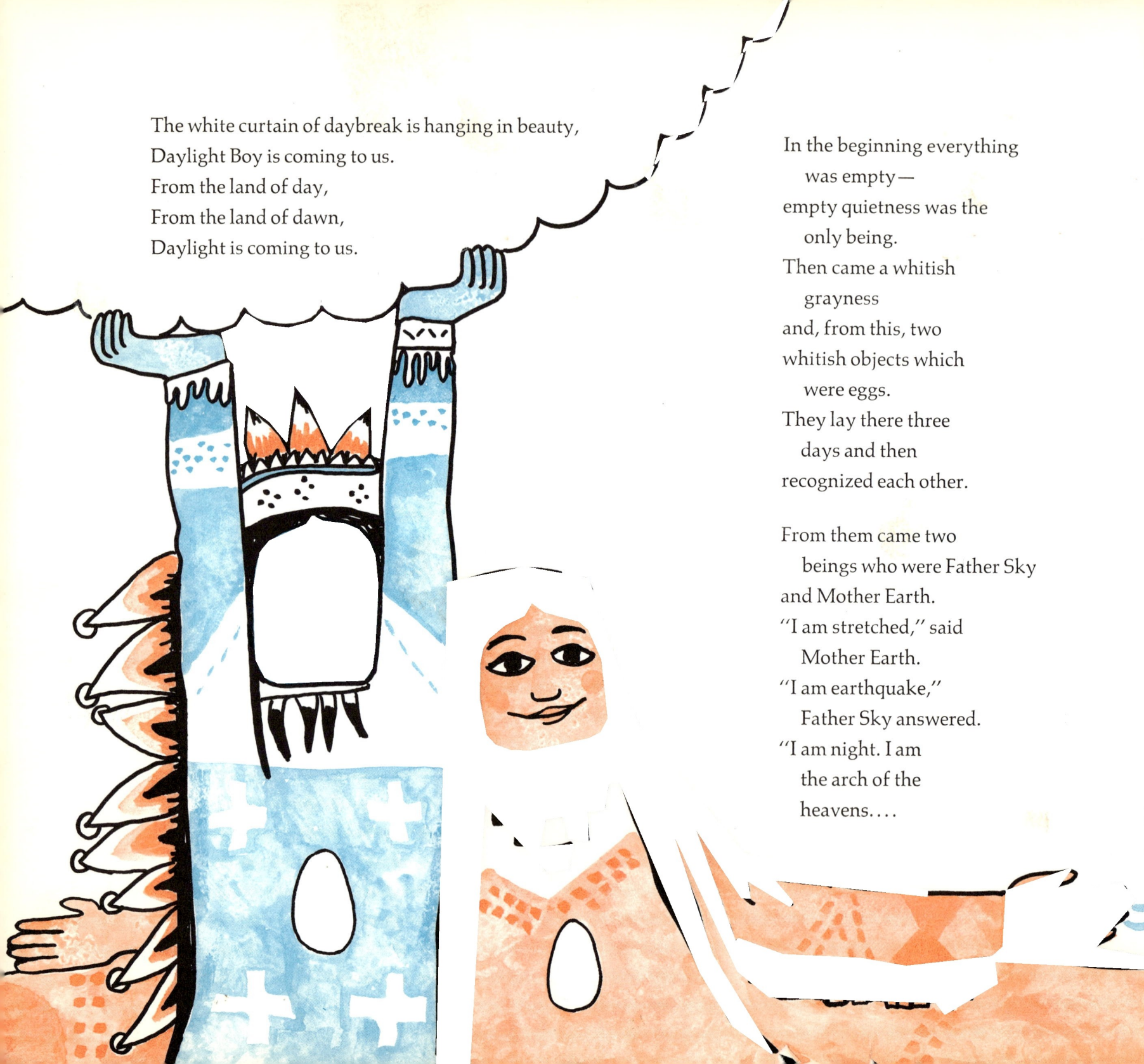

The white curtain of daybreak is hanging in beauty,
Daylight Boy is coming to us.
From the land of day,
From the land of dawn,
Daylight is coming to us.

In the beginning everything
 was empty—
empty quietness was the
 only being.
Then came a whitish
 grayness
and, from this, two
whitish objects which
 were eggs.
They lay there three
 days and then
recognized each other.

From them came two
 beings who were Father Sky
and Mother Earth.
"I am stretched," said
 Mother Earth.
"I am earthquake,"
 Father Sky answered.
"I am night. I am
 the arch of the
 heavens...."

"We sprang from salt water,
 a meeting of waves.

With a song
we were born,
startling the birds
into flight
while the seagulls
cried,
circling the air
and following
the strain of our paddles,
moving us
toward land....

Our people will not die."

I have made a baby board for you, my son;
May you grow to a great old age.
Of the sun's rays have I made the back,
Of black clouds have I made the blanket,
Of rainbow have I made the bow,
Of sunbeams have I made the side loops,
Of lightning have I made the lacings,
Of sun dogs have I made the footboard,
Of dawn have I made the covering,
Of black fog have I made the bed.

    Dawn Boy, give him many horses;
    Dawn Boy, give him many sheep.

Rivers flow.
The sea sings.
Oceans roar.
Tides rise.
Who am I?
A small pebble
On a giant shore;
Who am I
To ask who I am?
Isn't it enough to be?

When I was but a child,
I dreamed a wondrous dream.
I went upon a mountain;
There I fell asleep.
I heard a voice say,
"Now I will appear to you."
A buffalo said this to
    me, dreaming;
When I was but a child,
I dreamed this wondrous
    dream.

They say a herd of buffalo is
 coming,
It is here now!
Their blessing will come
 to us;
It is with us now!

The Sun, the Light of the world,
I hear him coming!
I see his face as he comes.
He makes the beings on earth
 happy
And they rejoice.

O Wakan-Tanka, I offer you
 this Light of light.
This sacred day you made the
 buffalo roam,
You have made a happy day for the
 world.
I offer all to you!

Indians of the Plains say, "Because the drum is round it represents the whole universe, and its steady, strong beat is the pulse, the heart, throbbing at the center of the universe. It is the voice of Wakan-Tanka. And this sound stirs us and helps us to understand the mystery and power of all things."

Travel I will and travel I must
To drive my sheep beyond the dust.
No signpost marks the reach of space,
No season stays upon earth's face.
Where only silence hears my cry,
Alone we go, my sheep and I.

Where is your grandfather, little lamb?
Where is your mother, little lamb?
They are coming. All are coming home.

Stir-ring spoon now have I found,
Wood-en spoon with han-dle round.
Stir-ring spoon now have I found,
Wood-en spoon with han-dle round,
   Lit-tle sweet-heart of mine.

Indian maple sugar,
I am going to cook and stir,
   Lit-tle sweet-heart of mine.

All for her this treasure,
It will give her pleasure,
   Lit-tle sweet-heart of mine.

When Spring came,
Leaves grew with a green fresh
feeling,
And the warmth of the sun
Was beginning to be felt,
And the Animals of the Earth
Awoke, breathing the fresh new
smell
Of life all over again.

It's like the wind,
Gently blowing,
Making love to everything
Before it moves on
Yet returning.

On the Tecolate fields,
the corn was growing green,
growing green.
I came,
I saw the tassels waving in the wind,
and I whistled softly for joy.

Come and sing!
Come and sing in the old way,
Come and make the juice grow strong
So the corn will grow,
The squash will grow,
The beans will grow.

Like a star I shine.
The animal, gazing, is fascinated
   by my light.
My war club resounds through
   the sky
To summon the animals
   to my call.

To my bow I say, be strong.
To my arrow I say, be swift.

To my arm I say, be strong.
To my eye I say, be sure.

Be strong, be swift, be sure
As the Children of the Sun.

O-ni-wa-ku-she? O-ni-wa-ku-she?
Where is lit-tle fox? Where is lit-tle fox?

   En-o-mi ka-wi-ya wa-ku-she.
There I see tracks of lit-tle fox.
   Da-da-min ne-o-wa wa-ku-she.
Now I catch up with him, lit-tle fox.

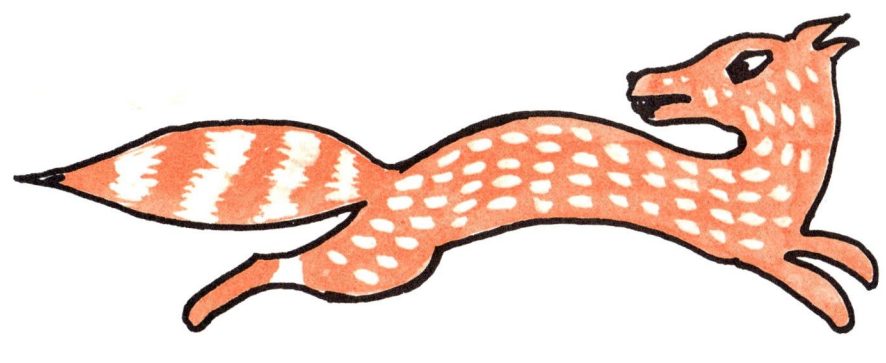

i stand on the rock
ho, bear!
beware of me!

i stand on the tree
ho, eagle!
beware of me!

i stand on the mountain
ho, enemy!
beware of me!

i stand in the camp
ho, chiefs!
beware of me!

here comes a bee!
i run and hide!
he would sting me!

Hoot Owl, my friend,
Gnaw the bowstring of my enemy
And make him helpless.

The snow has come at last,
Coming down in soft flakes,
Caressing my face with tenderness
As if it were telling me,
You are the first I've touched.

And as I walk along,
The snowflakes seem to sing
A song that has never been heard,
A song that has never been sung,
Unheard, unsung, except in my heart.

My life, my single tree—
We dance around you
All around the circle of the
    sky I hear the spirit's voice.
I walk upon half of the sky;
I am the crow, his skin is my
    body.

Tall Cedar Tree!
    Clap your hands
    and sing to me!
Si Si-em, thank you.
Si Si-em, thank you.

Tall Cedar Tree!
    Reach out your arms
    and shelter me,
Si Si-em, thank you.
Si Si-em, thank you.

Tall Cedar Tree,
    please let me forever be
    right by your loving side.
Si Si-em, thank you.
Si Si-em, thank you.

Then from the East a wind arose,
Well knowing whither it should blow....
All kinds of clouds together,
Their heads upreared
And with it they did go;
Pulling white feathers from their breasts,
they went.

The mountains pull at me,
The trees stroke my eyes,
The wind brushes by,
Pulling down the sky.

The flowers tug at me,
The streams wash me down,
Life drives at me,
I fall and hug the ground.

Hear the loud sound?
The thunderbirds draw near
   us in their mighty power.
Hear their voices!
The lightning flash is the
   gleaming of their terrible eyes.
The roll in the storm-swept
   sky
Is the noise of the
   thunderbirds' wings.

Softly so as not to wake the day too soon.
Clouds listen, pouting with rain, black.
Bolts of lightning scream with no shame
Bright flashes to show that heaven cries.
I'm glad to be safe inside—dry.

Just at daylight bluebird calls.
The bluebird has a voice;
He has a voice, his voice melodious,
His voice melodious that flows in gladness.
Bluebird calls. Bluebird calls.

    I wonder how it feels to fly
high in the sky...
    like a bird.

    I wonder how it feels to sit
on a nest...
    like a bird.

    I wonder how it feels to catch
a worm in the morning...
    like a bird.

    I feel funny...
maybe he is wondering
    how it feels to be like a man.

I go forth to move about the earth.
I go forth as the owl, wise and knowing.
I go forth as the eagle, powerful and bold.
I go forth as the dove, powerful and gentle.
I go forth to move about the earth
   in wisdom, courage, and peace.

The frog does not
Drink up
The pond in which he lives.

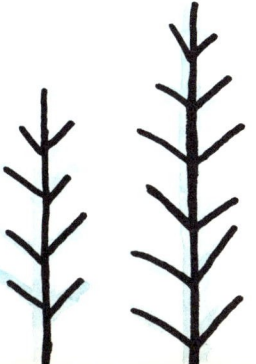

"Do not forget
 The Willows by the River Rain.
 Remember the Blue Mountains
 And the fire of Autumn treetops.

Remember the deer's flesh,
Fresh from the killing,
And the neigh of Pinto ponies,
Racing through the whispering grass."

In the house of long life, there I wander.
In the house of happiness, there I wander.
Beauty before me, with it I wander.
Beauty behind me, with it I wander.
Beauty below me, with it I wander.
Beauty all around me, with it I wander.
In old age traveling, with it I wander.
On the trail of beauty I am, with it I wander.

INDEX of first lines and tribal identification in order of appearance in the book.

Lo, the turquoise horse of Johano-Ai
(courtesy, Museum of Navaho Ceremonial Art, Inc., Santa Fe, New Mexico)

The white curtain of daybreak is hanging in beauty
(Navajo, as told to Doris Helander)

In the beginning everything was empty
(Mission Indians of California)

We sprang from salt water
(Makah, Sandra Johnson, Neah Bay, courtesy, *Argus* Magazine, Seattle)

I have made a baby board for you, my son
(Navajo, *Children of the People*, courtesy Harvard University Press, Leighton and Kluckhon)

Rivers flow
(Cherokee, Shirley Catt Lincoln)

With visible breath
(Oglala Sioux, *American Indians Sing*, Chas. Hofmann, courtesy John Day Company)

When I was but a child
(South Dakota Sioux, *ibid.*)

They say a herd of buffalo is coming
(Plains, *ibid.*)

Indians of the Plains say
(Plains, *ibid.*)

Travel I will and travel I must
(Navajo, as told to Doris Helander)

Where is your grandfather, little lamb?
(Navajo, *ibid.*)

Stir-ring spoon now have I found
(Iroquois, Great Lakes, courtesy Cooperative Recreation Service, Inc., Delaware, Ohio)

When Spring came
(Tlingit, Darrell St. Clair, Anchorage, Alaska)

On the Tecolate fields
(Pima, courtesy Bureau of Indian Affairs, U.S. Interior Dept.)

Come and sing
(Pueblo, *ibid.*)

Like a star I shine
(Chippewa)

To my bow I say, be strong
(Navajo as told to Doris Helander)

O-ni-wa-ku-she? O-ni-wa-ku-she
(Chippewa, courtesy Cooperative Recreation Service, Inc., Delaware, Ohio)

i stand on the rock
(Western Cherokee, Norman Russell, Central State College)

Hoot Owl, my friend
(Pueblo, courtesy Bureau of Indian Affairs, U.S. Interior Dept.)

The snow has come at last
(Navajo, Tommy Smith, courtesy *Argus* Magazine)

My life, my single tree
(Chippewa, *American Indians Sing*, Chas. Hofmann, courtesy John Day Company)

Tall Cedar Tree
(Northwest coast, Pauline Covington, courtesy *Argus* Magazine, Seattle)

Then from the East a wind arose
(Papago, courtesy Bureau of Indian Affairs, U.S. Interior Dept.)

The mountains pull at me
(Cherokee, Carl Lloyd Owle)

Hear the loud sound
(Chippewa, *American Indians Sing*, Chas. Hofmann, courtesy John Day Company)

Softly so as not to wake the day too soon
(Cherokee, Shirley Catt Lincoln)

Just at daylight bluebird calls
(Navajo)

I wonder how it feels to fly
(Yakima, Earl Thompson, courtesy, *Argus* Magazine, Seattle)

I go forth to move about the earth
(Papago, Alonzo Lopez, *ibid.*)

The frog does not
(Navajo proverb)

Do not forget
(Northwest coast, David Wolf, courtesy *Argus* Magazine)

In the house of long life, there I wander
(Navajo)

My horse be swift in flight
(Sioux, *American Indians Sing*, Chas. Hofmann, courtesy John Day Company)

FLORA HOOD

grew up in the South, where she taught school and worked for several years on a newspaper. During World War II she joined the Associated Press and after the war began a long association with the Bureau of Indian Affairs. She was first placed in Arizona to teach English to Navajos, then was transferred to two Pueblo Indian villages in New Mexico. She also spent considerable time on the Eastern Cherokee reservation. Her last job with the BIA was teaching in an isolated Navajo day school in Utah. When she decided to retire early to write, her Navajo friends helped her move to Albuquerque, where she lived for several years. Her numerous writings reflect her wide travels in America and her deep and loving relationships with the people with whom she has worked. Miss Hood now makes her home in South Carolina.

MARYLOU REIFSNYDER

was born in San Francisco. She worked with the U.S. Forest Service in Berkeley before becoming the museum assistant and assistant registrar of the Yale Art Gallery. She has long had an interest in Indian folk art, and one of her two daughters has worked with the Navajos on a reservation in Arizona. Mrs. Reifsnyder lives in Connecticut with her husband, who is a professor of forest meteorology at Yale, and th   young son, Gawain.

My horse be swift in flight,
Even like a bird;
My horse be swift in flight,
Bear me now in safety
Far from the enemy's arrows,
And you shall be rewarded
With streamers and ribbons red.